EVERY
BUILDING
HAS A HISTORY

Andrew Langley

Heinemann
LIBRARY
Chicago, Illinois

Edited by Andrew Farrow, James Benefield, and Adrian
Vigliano
Designed by Tim Bond
Original illustrations © Capstone Global Library Ltd 2014
Picture research by Liz Alexander
Originated by Capstone Global Library Ltd
Production by Victoria Fitzgerald

Printed and bound in China

17 16 15 14 13
10 9 8 7 6 5 4 3 2 1

Library of Congress Cataloging-in-Publication Data
Langley, Andrew, 1949-
  Every building has a history / Andrew Langley.
    pages cm—(Everything has a history)
  Includes bibliographical references and index.
  ISBN 978-1-4329-9583-6 (hb)—ISBN 978-1-4329-9588-1
(pb) 1. Architecture—Juvenile literature. 2. Architecture
and history—Juvenile literature. 3. History—Research—
Juvenile literature. 4. History—Methodology—Juvenile
literature. I. Title.

  NA2555.L36 2014
  907.2—dc23   2013017189

Acknowledgments

We would like to thank the following for permission to
reproduce photographs: Alamy pp. 19 (© Nick Scott),
23 (© INTERFOTO), 27 (© Jan Wlodarczyk), 33 (© Library
of Congress / Photri Images), 35 (© Kevin Shields), 37 (©
The Print Collector), pp. 41t, 43 (© Adrian Sherratt), 49 (©
Everett Collection Historical), 53 (© Steve Vidler), Corbis pp.
29R, 46 (Peter Adams/AWL Images), 57 (Peet Simard), Getty
Images pp. 17 (David Clapp), 29L (Andrew Holt), 51 (Edwin
Levick), 54 (Bentley Archive/Popperfoto); Laura Leibman/
Jewish Atlantic World Website and Archive p. 11; Newport
Historical Society p. 9; Shutterstock p. 21 (© S.Borisov);
Superstock pp. 5 (Robert Harding Picture Library), 13
(Universal Images Group), 15 (Photononstop), 24 (Gonzalo
Azumendi/age footstock), 39 (Science and Society);
Newcastle City Library p. 31; The National Archives 41b (ref
E31/2/1 f88).

Cover photograph: Shopping area of Eurostar terminal
at St. Pancras station reproduced with the permission of
Shutterstock (Axiom Photographic/Design Pics); St. Pancras
station in construction reproduced with the permission
of Shutterstock (Antonio Abriginani); St. Pancras station
in 2011 reproduced with the permission of Shutterstock
(© Patrick Wang); St. Pancras International in London
reproduced with the permission of Shutterstock (© Gary
Blakeley).

CONTENTS

Some words are shown in **bold,** like this. You can find out what they mean by looking in the glossary.

STORIES IN STONE

We are surrounded by buildings. Most of them look ordinary, yet they may have surprising stories to tell. How and why were they built? Who lived in them? What were their links with other events? This book looks at examples of building types and helps you discover these hidden tales for yourself. It explains basic research techniques and guides you to the best places to find revealing **evidence**. Indeed, buildings do not necessarily tell us much about the past without evidence—and, sometimes, the buildings themselves inspire the search for this evidence.

Remote Ruins

A building stands in a wooded valley in England. Nobody lives here. There are no roofs or doors—just soaring stone walls pierced with tall windows. It is a ruin. Yet Rievaulx Abbey was once one of the biggest and wealthiest **monasteries** in Great Britain.

What does this building tell us about its history? First, this was clearly a place devoted to the Christian religion—probably a community of monks. It also looks very old. Some research into architectural style would show that it was built almost 900 years ago. Finally, it must have been very prosperous. There are the remains of over 70 buildings on the site, including the massive church itself. A study of historic maps would confirm that the abbey grounds also held large areas of woodland and farmland in the surrounding countryside.

What Happened Next?

If it was so successful, why is Rievaulx an empty ruin today? A wealthy abbey must have contained many beautiful and valuable **artifacts**. What happened to them? To answer this, you need to know some British history. In the 1530s, England's King Henry VIII ordered the closure of all monasteries in England. The monks were forced to leave, and Rievaulx Abbey was sold to the duke of Rutland. He quickly stripped away all valuable materials.

Today, Rievaulx Abbey looks well cared for, with many rebuilt walls and grassed areas cleared of debris (loose fragments of something that has been destroyed). This is because the abbey is now a national **monument**, attracting thousands of visitors every year.

The huge columns and arches of Rievaulx Abbey have been rebuilt and restored, and the ground has been cleared.

How Do We Know the Story of Rievaulx Abbey?

The abbey's history stretches over nearly 900 years. During this long period, a lot of evidence has built up. Here are the key places where you would start your research into the story of Rievaulx:

- The ruins themselves: By studying the layout of the remaining walls and buildings, and the materials they are made of, you can learn a lot about how and why the abbey was built, and about monastic life in the Middle Ages.

- The objects found on the site: Over 4,000 artifacts were dug up during the restoration. These are now stored in a museum in the nearby town of Helmsley, England.

- The writings of the monks: Monks kept records of their farming and other financial dealings. There is also a biography of Rievaulx's most famous abbot (leader), Saint Aelred.

- The work of later historians: Since the 1750s, several people have examined the site and written detailed descriptions of it, with drawings, plans, and (later) photographs.

Research Basics

Rievaulx Abbey is just one example of a building that can teach us a lot of history, but there are countless more throughout the world. What kind of building would you like to research? How do you begin finding out about your subject? It may be an individual school assignment or part of a class project. You may want to know more about the background of your own home. Whatever it is, you need to make connections between the building you see today and what happened there in the past.

There are so many methods and sources for research that you can easily get confused or frustrated. Start by deciding what questions you want to ask about key themes and issues. Then look at the basic tools needed to answer them. Once you have the answers, you can evaluate them to see how they will fit into your final presentation.

Looking for Information

Where do you find your evidence? The most obvious place is the building itself. But there are some other obvious starting points:

- The library: Libraries give you access to maps, DVDs, newspaper **archives**, and many other sources, as well as books of all kinds.
- The Internet: The material you want is there somewhere—the only difficulty is finding exactly what you want.
- Museums: Specialized and local history museums contain a wealth of objects, which can tell you a lot about an area and its development.
- Your own eyes and ears: Listen to what local people have to say. For example, you could talk to curators of local museums (these are the people who manage the museum collections) or local historians, or ask family members what they know about a building.

Learning the Language

Like most things, research has its own jargon (special language). Here are some of the basic terms you are likely to come across when you begin:

- The information you are looking for is called evidence. This is the raw material, made up of facts and other elements that provide a firm base for your project.

- Evidence comes from two main sources: The first type is **primary sources**, from the time of the events you are studying. These are usually created by people who were there and can describe the scene directly. They can include diaries, letters, eyewitness accounts, and photographs. Future researchers may refer to current news reports as primary evidence.

- **Secondary sources** are the second kind of source. They are produced later. These are new accounts or **interpretations** of the events by historians using primary or other secondary source material. Secondary sources include the Internet, history textbooks, biographies, encyclopedias, and documentary films.

As the evidence piles up, you can easily be swamped by facts, figures, and other material. Graphic organizers are tools that can help you keep things in order and stay focused on your topic. There are many different kinds of organizers, including charts, diagrams, concept webs, and tables.

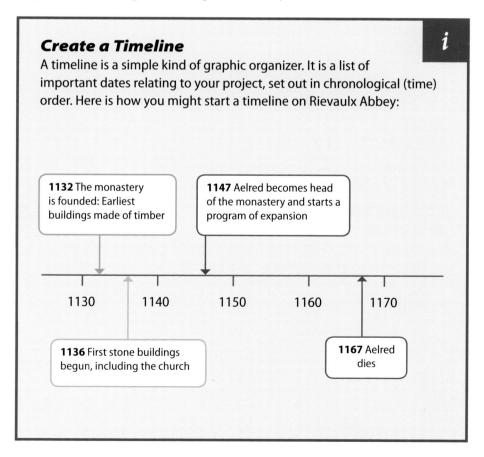

Create a Timeline
i

A timeline is a simple kind of graphic organizer. It is a list of important dates relating to your project, set out in chronological (time) order. Here is how you might start a timeline on Rievaulx Abbey:

1132 The monastery is founded: Earliest buildings made of timber

1147 Aelred becomes head of the monastery and starts a program of expansion

1130   1140   1150   1160   1170

1136 First stone buildings begun, including the church

1167 Aelred dies

Number 42 Pope Street is an old-fashioned home near the waterfront in Newport, Rhode Island. It has a brownstone ground floor and a **clapboard** upper floor. It looks old, but it is so ordinary that you would pass it by without a second glance. Yet detective work by local historians proved that this house has a dramatic link with the slave trade.

Window on the Past

In 2012, the Newport Historical Society obtained a precious piece of primary material. It was a letter from a man named Occramar Marycoo, who had spent most of his life in Newport. In October 1821, he wrote to his niece, Sarah, who lived in Alexandria, Virginia. The letter began, "I received yours dated June 25 with great pleasure; for as cold water to a thirsted soul so is good news from a far country: I rejoice to hear that there are two colored churches there [in Alexandria]."

This letter gives us a tiny glimpse into the private life of an extraordinary man. Occramar Marycoo worked as a slave in Newport. Yet due to his talent, hard work, and good luck, he managed to become a free man. He also purchased his own family house—an amazing achievement for a former black slave in that period. The house was number 42 Pope Street.

The Transatlantic Slave Trade

i

Europeans began importing slaves from Africa to the Americas in the early 1500s. Among the major traders were the British, who soon ruled a group of new colonies on North America's east coast. Merchants bought slaves in central African ports and shipped them to different parts of North America or the Caribbean. Slaves worked on tobacco and sugar plantations, or in mills, stores, and houses. When British rule ended after the Revolutionary War (1775–1783), U.S. merchants carried on the trade. By the time slavery was **abolished** in the United States in 1865, over 11 million Africans had been transported across the Atlantic.

Occramar Marycoo's letter to his niece, written in 1821, was bought by the Newport Historical Society in 2012.

From Ghana to Rhode Island

Occramar Marycoo was born in Ghana, Africa, in 1746. He was sold into slavery at the age of 14. Packed on a ship with other slaves, he crossed the Atlantic and arrived in Newport in about 1760. He was sold to Caleb Gardner, a naval captain who lived in the town.

Gardner was a merchant and shipowner who carried cargo to China and South Asian countries. He also had a house near the harbor, where Marycoo worked as a house slave. Gardner changed his new slave's name to "Newport Gardner," though Marycoo continued using his original name throughout his life.

Where Should I Look?

If you visit Newport, you may be able to see Occramar Marycoo's house (it is now run as a bed-and-breakfast). Anyone farther away will have to rely on books and the Internet. Type "Rhode Island History" into an Internet search engine, and you will find several well-illustrated, useful sites, including one for the Rhode Island Historical Society.

Music and Marriage

Very quickly, Marycoo showed he had remarkable talents. By the age of 18, he had learned two new languages: English and French. He had also become a skilled musician and had composed his first pieces of music. In the 1780s, he married Limas, another slave, and together they had five children.

But he was still a slave, and in law this meant that he was part of his master's property. Like other slaves, he yearned to be set free or to save enough money to purchase his freedom. Then, in 1791, something astonishing happened. With several friends, Marycoo bought a lottery ticket and won nearly $2,000, a huge sum in those days (comparable to some of the biggest prizes in nationwide lotteries today). With his share, he was able to buy freedom for himself and his family. There was enough left over to buy a new home—on Pope Street.

A Free Man

Marycoo now had his liberty and a home of his own. He supported his growing family by giving music and singing lessons. In fact, he is recognized today as one of the nation's first-ever black music teachers and composers. Among his best-known works is a song called "Crooked Shanks" and a piece for the choir called "Promise".

But his life had its tragic side, too. In 1790, Marycoo's daughter Silva died. We know this because that year he bought a headstone for her grave in Newport's burial ground for Africans, which was known locally as "God's Little Acre." He paid for it with ten **bushels** of potatoes (about 600 pounds, or 270 kilograms). The purchase was recorded in the accounts of a Newport mason named John Stevens.

Working for His People

Marycoo devoted much of his life to his religion and to improving the lives of his fellow African Americans in Newport. While still a slave in 1780, he had helped to found the African Union Society (AUS). Black people at this time were barred from most parts of white society, including churches and schools. The AUS was a mutual aid association for black men. This means it supported its members in times of hardship, paying for their schooling and health. Marycoo was the society's secretary.

With his savings and winnings, Marycoo was able to buy this substantial brownstone and clapboard house on Pope Street in 1791. Today, it provides bed-and-breakfast accommodation.

Conflicting Evidence

i

Sometimes you find your sources do not agree with each other. One source may give a piece of evidence as a fact, but another source provides a different fact. The story of Mr. Marycoo provides several examples of conflicting evidence:

- Some sources call him Occramar. Others call him Occramer, or even Occarmar.

- Some sources say he bought his freedom with part of the cash he won in the lottery. However, another source states that Caleb Gardner overheard him praying for freedom from slavery and was so moved that he made him a free man on the spot.

Who is right and who is wrong? We do not know for certain. It is best to use evidence that is backed up by two or more reliable primary sources. But if both sets of facts seem credible, then cite both versions, pointing this out.

A Church for Black People

Marycoo continued to work hard to provide better conditions for African Americans in Newport. The African Union Society held its services in a church used by white worshippers on Division Street. There was also a school here for African American children, which Marycoo helped to run. In 1805, he set up a similar mutual society for black women.

Both societies grew, and in 1824, Marycoo founded the Colored Union Church. This was the first free black church in Newport, "where the Negro might worship God without segregation." By now, they had the church building on Division Street to themselves, since the white congregation had moved elsewhere.

Back to Africa

Marycoo was now an old man of 78. But he still had the energy to join in one last big project. This was known as the "Back to Africa" Movement. Its aim was to encourage ex-slaves to return to Africa as **missionaries** and attempt to convert the people there to Christianity.

In January 1826, Marycoo set sail from Boston, with his sons and several neighbors. Their ship carried books, tools, food, and even a printing press, all thanks to money raised by the Union Colored Church. The party landed in Liberia, in Africa, in February. However, by the end of the same year, many had died of local diseases. Among the dead was Marycoo, who fulfilled his dream of being buried in African soil.

What Is Missing?

But this has been just a bare outline. There are many gaps in Marycoo's life, which you may be able to fill in with more research. For instance, what more can you find out about his house? Is the music he composed still being played? What does it sound like?

There is also the background story. Marycoo lived through a dramatic time in U.S. history, with events including the Revolutionary War, the expansion of the new United States, the growth of the cotton industry, and the beginning of the campaign to end slavery. How did these events affect life in Newport? How much do you think Marycoo would have known about some of these events?

Conditions on slave ships were horrifying. A large proportion of slaves usually died during each voyage, due to disease, starvation, or from general bad treatment.

Making a Connection: Why Were There Slaves in Rhode Island?

Most slaves worked on farms in the South and the Caribbean, where sugar was the most valuable crop. Yet Newport, far away in the Northeast, with no sugar plantations, was an important port on the slave route. Why was this? Here's a clue: sugar can be made into rum. When Marycoo arrived in Newport in the 1760s, there were 22 rum factories. And rum could be used to buy slaves from African traders. See what you can find out to fill in the gaps. Try web sites about slavery in the area, such as **www.slavenorth.com/rhodeisland.htm** or **www.colonialcemetery.com/newporthistory.htm**

YOUR HOME

Everyone grows up in a home, and every home has a history. Some have a sensational past. Take, for example, the nice old house on Osage Street in Denver, Colorado, bought by Matt Feeney in 2012. He was demolishing a wall when he found canvas packages taped to the back, filled with explosives. Feeney later discovered the house had belonged to a criminal gang in the 1970s.

Questions to Ask

Few houses contain stories as scary as this, but most have something interesting to tell us. Old homes have long histories. Concrete apartment buildings and modern houses, of course, have much shorter ones. But that does not necessarily make them less interesting. See what strange secrets you can uncover about the building you know best.

Start with a list of basic questions you want to answer. First, you need to set your home in time and space: when was it built, and where does it stand (which county and town or city)? Then you can get down to the details. What materials is the house made of? Who lived here before you and your family? What was on the site before the house was built?

Finding Answers

You are looking for information about one very specific, and probably very ordinary, location. You are not likely to find what you want in history books or on web sites (unless someone very famous lived in your home). Instead, you will need to tackle three types of research: 1) looking at documents, 2) looking at the building, and 3) talking to people.

Celebrity Homes
i

Has anyone famous lived in your house? If so, there may be a plaque on the outside wall. Plaques are used in many countries to show a link between a building and a famous person. These help add a sense of history to what could otherwise seem like ordinary buildings and neighborhoods.

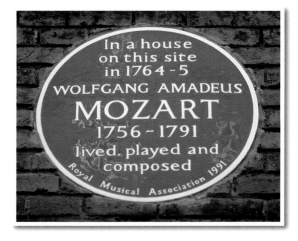

Sometimes the link between a famous person and a building is tiny. The London house where the composer Mozart lived for a few months has been knocked down and replaced by another house.

Documentary Evidence

There is a huge range of paperwork and other records that may help you. Here are a few of the most valuable sources of information:

- Libraries often have a local history section.

- Local museums contain varied and often surprising material.

- A huge number of old documents and maps are now available online.

- Your local churches, synagogues, and other religious institutions may have old photos and other images, as well as fascinating clues to the past in gravestones and their inscriptions.

- Regional newspapers may let you use their libraries of clippings (interesting extracts) and view back issues (previous editions).

- Local archives and records offices can contain a wealth of material, including **censuses** (records of local populations, made every 10 years), voter registration lists (lists of people who can vote in elections), and family papers such as birth, marriage, and death certificates.

- Real estate attorneys are qualified legal experts who prepare the paperwork for buying and selling houses. They may have the original title documents (which prove someone's right to own a property) to your house.

- Recorder of deeds: Find out where your local recorder of deeds office is located. This office will have extensive records related to real estate ownership.

Looking At the Building

The most important primary source of all is the house or building itself! After all, no two buildings are the same, and each one has something special and unique to tell you. These are a few of the major areas to look at:

• The outside: Examine the shape of the building, including the line of the roof and the placing of the windows and doors.

• The outside walls: A change in brick or stone course thickness may show where the building was extended. There may be dates or identifying marks carved on the outside wall by the builder.

• The style of windows, chimneys, and other features often indicate the period when the house was constructed.

• The inside walls: How many layers of paint or wallpaper are there? The oldest layers could be the most interesting.

• Unplastered areas inside, such as the attic or the basement: Exposed timber or brickwork might not have been touched for many years.

• The site: How far is your home from the center of the town or city? As a very rough rule, the further from the center often means the newer the house.

• The materials used to build the house: Are the walls stone, brick, or concrete? What is the roof made of? Did these materials come from a local source?

Organize Your Sources *i*

A source chart is a simple kind of graphic organizer. It has three columns: the first for recording useful facts, figures, and quotations; the second for noting the source where you found it; and the third for any page, web address, or reference detail.

Name: John Smith	Topic: My home	
Information	**Source**	**Reference**
The front wall has two different sizes of bricks	My own observation	–
The house is 2.5 miles from the town center	Local map	Garmin Topo US/ Great Lakes SD
My street was built in 1927	County Records Office	www.statearchives.us/ michigan.htm

What does the outside of this house in England tell you? It is built with a timber frame that looks very old. The windows have leaded bars. The upper floors (on the right) jut over the lower ones. It was actually built in the 14th century.

Ask the Experts

The history of houses is a big and complex subject. You will need help from expert historians to figure out what the clues mean. Consult books such as *A Field Guide to American Houses* by Virginia McAlester and others (New York: Knopf, 1984), web sites such as **architecture.about.com/od/periodsstyles/ig/House-Styles/**, or just browse the architecture or building sections of the library.

Research Road Show: The Animals of Bartons End

When George Ordish bought a Tudor farmhouse called Bartons End in Kent, England, he began researching its history. He was soon fascinated by the nonhuman inhabitants throughout the centuries. He looked at the physical evidence (for instance, holes bored by beetles in old timbers) and studied the kinds of insects and animals living in the area. With this, and mathematical calculation, he guessed that his family and pets shared the house with mice and a few birds, not to mention hundreds of beetles, spiders, fleas, bedbugs, flies, cockroaches, and moths. Their ancestors had lived there for nearly 500 years!

Talking to People

Many people might know about your house, including your family. By talking to them, you may be able to get useful information that could not be found in books or other documentary records. But act sensitively and carefully, because not everyone will be willing to be interviewed. Make sure you explain what you are doing in your project, and have a list of clear questions to ask. Here are some people you could approach:

- Neighbors, who may have lived nearby for many years: Neighbors' memories may stretch back for several decades, so they will be able to tell you about the recent history of the area, and your home in particular.

- Previous residents: Previous residents may be difficult to trace because they have moved to a different area. If you locate their address, you could put your questions in a letter or an e-mail.

- Real estate agents: Real estate agents who have been involved in the sale of the house at some time in the past may have records, pictures, or memories of the building. Start by contacting the company that was dealing with the house when you moved in.

- Local history groups, which study the area in detail: Members of local history groups may already have done a large amount of neighborhood research and may even have written books about local history. For contact names, ask at your library.

Where Should I Look?: Looking for Something In the Yard

The yard is one part of the home where you can try to do all the research yourself. (If you do not have a yard, join a history or **archaeology** group that conducts local excavations.) At some stage, your yard may be dug up or rearranged. If this happens, look carefully through the newly dug soil. There could be all sorts of objects buried here, such as bottles, broken china, decorated tiles, pieces of clay, and even old toys. Sometimes the finds are much more dramatic, such as finding valuables or even bones!

Making a Connection: Change of Use

Was your home always a residence? Many buildings started out as something very different—stores, restaurants, chapels, train stations, schools, or barns—and were then converted into homes when they fell out of use. Some very big buildings, such as factories, warehouses, or mansions, have been divided up into apartments. More unusual homes started out as aircraft, water towers, industrial packing cases, or even grain silos. For example, Joanne Ussery, in Benoit, Missouri, made her home out of an old Boeing 727 airliner!

Some unusual buildings are converted into homes. This is an example: it used to be a lighthouse! Can you imagine living in a place like this? What other unusual buildings can people live in?

REDISCOVERING THE PARTHENON

A flat outcrop of rock towers over Athens, Greece's capital. This is the Acropolis, or "High City." And in the middle of the rock stands the Parthenon, one of the oldest and most beautiful buildings in the world. Built over 2,400 years ago, it is a **symbol** of the greatness of ancient Greece, the birthplace of **democracy**. But how do we know what the Parthenon was for and how has it been used during its long history? Even today, archaeologists from the Acropolis Restoration Service are working there to find fresh answers.

The Parthenon Today

If you visit the Parthenon or look at a recent photograph, you will see a large rectangular building made of light-colored marble. It looks like an ancient temple—which is exactly what it was. The roof is held up by 46 tall columns, spaced regularly around the outside. Inside are two big rooms, also supported by columns.

However, the Parthenon is not complete. It has been badly damaged, because most of the roof has disappeared and there are many gaps and broken slabs. Around the columns lie piles of stone and pieces of sculpture, which have clearly fallen from the building. You may also see scaffolding, cranes, and other machinery and tools used by workers repairing this magnificent structure.

What Did It Look Like In Ancient Times?

The Parthenon today seems a solemn, elegant place, despite the debris. But when it was first completed, it looked very different. One room was a treasury filled with gold and other precious objects. The other contained a massive sculpture of Athena, the **patron goddess** of the city. It was made of wood covered in gold and ivory and was 40 feet (12 meters) high. Other statues and carvings may also have been brightly painted.

How do we know this? The treasure and the great statue disappeared centuries ago. Only the empty rooms are left. The only evidence comes from the work of ancient writers. For instance, the statue of Athena was described by a visitor in about 150 CE. A Greek traveler named Pausanias wrote the very first guidebook to Greece, and in it, he recorded details of the Parthenon and its carvings. This is the only eyewitness account of what the interior looked like in the **classical** period.

The Parthenon was built on a huge flat hill called the Acropolis. The people of Athens used the hill as a refuge and stronghold if they were attacked. Although most buildings on the Acropolis are now damaged, there is ongoing conservation work to try to restore it to its former glory.

Zoom In: The Golden Age of Athens

Work on the Parthenon began in 447 BCE. It was one of many grand buildings erected at the time, intended to celebrate the great achievements of the Athenians. They had developed the first democratic system of government, in which citizens elected their rulers in a free vote. They had also saved themselves from invasion by defeating armies and navies sent by the mighty Persian Empire in an amazing series of battles between 490 and 479 BCE. The period became known as the city's Golden Age. Aside from the Acropolis, remnants of this time— including now-ruined buildings—can be found all over Greece and the surrounding area.

The Parthenon Transformed

Few great buildings have been altered and damaged as much as the Parthenon—and survived. In its very long existence, it has changed:

- Into a ruin: First, there was a disastrous fire, probably in about 250 CE. There are no written records of this event, but archaeologists have figured out the extent of the damage by examining scorched fragments of stone and tiles. These show that the roof and almost everything inside was destroyed (including the giant statue of Athena). The heat cracked marble pillars and sculptures.

- Into a church: The Romans conquered ancient Greece in 146 BCE, and it became part of their huge empire. After the Roman emperors became Christians, they banned **pagan** worship (of the old gods and goddesses). Sometime after 500 CE, the Parthenon was converted into a Christian church, complete with bell tower. Many of the stone carvings were deliberately damaged, because they showed pagan scenes. You can see these in the new Acropolis Museum, near the Parthenon.

- Into a mosque: The Turks took control of Greece in 1458, after capturing Athens, and turned the Acropolis into a military base. They also converted the church inside the Parthenon into a mosque. Christian objects were removed, paintings were covered in whitewash, and the bell tower became a **minaret**. The base and the stairway of this can still be seen.

- And back into a ruin: The Turks also used the Parthenon as a place to store their gunpowder. In 1687, Venetian forces attacked Athens and bombarded the Acropolis. The Parthenon was hit by over 700 cannonballs (you can still see the marks today). The gunpowder exploded, killing 300 people and causing major damage to the building. The interior was wrecked, and many pillars and carvings were smashed to pieces.

Where Should I Look?: Ancient Sources

The vast majority of primary sources from ancient Greece have been lost or destroyed over the centuries. Researchers have to rely on what has survived. This includes books by Pausanias, Plutarch, Pliny, and other writers, as well as the remains of art found at major Greek sites such as the Acropolis. Look for history books about the period that may have extracts from these works translated into English.

In 1707, well-known Venetian artist Francesco Fanelli made this drawing of the 1687 explosion. His picture included the minaret, converted from the bell tower by the Turks.

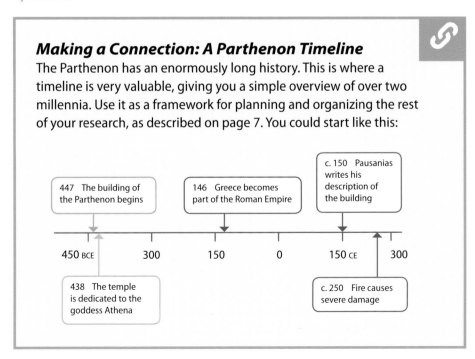

Making a Connection: A Parthenon Timeline

The Parthenon has an enormously long history. This is where a timeline is very valuable, giving you a simple overview of over two millennia. Use it as a framework for planning and organizing the rest of your research, as described on page 7. You could start like this:

447 The building of the Parthenon begins

146 Greece becomes part of the Roman Empire

c. 150 Pausanias writes his description of the building

450 BCE   300   150   0   150 CE   300

438 The temple is dedicated to the goddess Athena

c. 250 Fire causes severe damage

The Looting of the Acropolis

For nearly 150 years, the Parthenon remained a wreck, with only a few columns standing at each end and a hole in the middle of the building. In fact, the damage grew worse. Local people took away fallen stones and ground up marble to make cement. With these materials, they built simple houses, many of which crowded around the ruins on the Acropolis.

Worse still, foreign visitors to the site looted statues and other carvings and took them home. Small fragments to whole pieces of sculpture were stolen in this way. Wealthy art collectors paid agents to select and send the most attractive pieces. These can now be found in museums and other collections all over the world.

The Elgin Marbles

The most famous incident was the removal of vast amounts of material by the Scottish earl of Elgin (also known as Lord Elgin) between 1801 and 1805. Some of it had already fallen off, but many other pieces were hacked from the building with chisels. These included about half of the carved frieze (a broad horizontal strip above the columns) and large statues from the **pediments**.

This horse's head was carved to fit into a corner of the Parthenon pediment. It is one of the pieces taken by Lord Elgin and is on display at the British Museum in London.

All of these were shipped to England. The "Elgin Marbles," as they became known, were first put on public display in 1817. Some people were horrified by the removal of the sculptures. The poet Lord Byron called Elgin a vandal. They can still be seen today, in their own specially designed gallery, at the British Museum in London. The frieze, and the carefully arranged pediment figures, are among the most popular exhibits in the museum. More fragments from the Parthenon, taken by other collectors at the same time, can be found in other cities including Paris, France, and Copenhagen, Denmark.

Making a Connection: Should the Elgin Marbles Be Returned to Greece?

Ever since Elgin's time, there have been bitter arguments over whether the Elgin Marbles should stay in the United Kingdom or be given back to the Greeks. The debate was raised again when the Greek government built a new museum on the Acropolis to display the treasures of the building (which was completed in 2007). Gaps were left to show the pieces that were still in British hands. What do you think? Here are some of the arguments:

For Returning:

- The Parthenon carvings are a single work of art; therefore, they should be displayed together in one place.
- The British do not legally own the Marbles.
- Several other countries have already returned their looted fragments to Athens.

Against Returning:

- The Marbles have been preserved much better in London, safe from pollution and other threats in Athens.
- If all cultural objects were given back to their country of origin, some museums would soon be empty.
- At least half of the treasures of the Parthenon have been lost, so they can never be exhibited as a whole. You can learn more by looking at web sites such as **www.americanchronicle.com/articles/view/92096**

A New Start

The Greeks won their independence from the Turks in 1829, after a long struggle. At last, they could regain some of the glory of their classical past by restoring and studying ancient monuments such as the Parthenon. For the first time in its history, the Parthenon officially became an important site, and it was put under the control of the new Greek Archaeological Service.

Work on the Acropolis began in 1835. The military barracks, the minaret, and other houses were demolished. Layers of garbage, rubble, and topsoil were dug out. Archaeologists sorted and examined the masses of fallen stone blocks, making several major discoveries. For example, they found traces of a previous Parthenon on the site, which had been destroyed by the invading Persians in 480 BCE.

The Parthenon Rises Again...

In 1898, a much bigger project started—reconstructing the Parthenon. For over three decades, the engineer Nikolaos Balanos rebuilt the walls, columns, and the roof. His work created the temple, which has become one of the most recognizable images in the world.

But was this actually what the original Parthenon looked like? Many historians believed that Balanos had gotten it wrong. He had simply used his imagination to reconstruct the building, rather than thorough research. Worse still, he had repaired many broken blocks with iron clamps, which had started to rust and split the stone.

...and Again

So, in 1975, a brand new agency was set up, called the Acropolis Restoration Service. This began a fresh program of restoration and **conservation** over the whole site. Every single stone was identified and marked, and all the sculptures were moved to a new museum, with **replica** casts in their place.

The Parthenon itself is being rebuilt very carefully. The iron clamps are being replaced with ones made of titanium (which does not rust). Each block is being laid in its original position, wherever possible. All this painstaking work is supported by the expert knowledge of archaeologists and other scholars.

Various reconstruction and restoration attempts have been made at the Parthenon since 1898. However, the site is still open to the public, since it is an important tourist and cultural destination in Greece.

Research Road Show:
There's No Tool Like an Old Tool

The conservation team learned a lot about the astonishing skills of the ancient Greek builders. For a start, they probably had better tools. Team leader Manolis Korres analyzed the surface marks and concluded that the original masons used chisels and axes that were sharper and tougher than anything available today. With these, they could carve marble more than twice as quickly as modern craftworkers. This helps explain how they were able to put a remarkable finishing touch to the stone. Every marble surface was patterned with millions of tiny chisel blows in neat rows covering walls, floors, and columns. The effect was to disguise flaws in the stone. Korres says this "may have taken as much as a quarter of the total construction time expended on the monument."

Do you know the secrets hidden in your school? The staff and students at Teesside High School thought they did. Then, in 2011, a tree blew down. It revealed a hole in the ground—and beneath this was a buried building. Research showed it was an air raid shelter built during World War II (1939–1945). The shelter will be used as a living history project, to teach students about life during wartime.

Stories In Schools

You spend a lot of time inside a school. But how much do you actually know about the buildings? Have you ever imagined what they might tell you about the school's history? There may be lots of fascinating evidence to discover.

You can learn a lot from the structure of your school and how it has changed over time. Locate maps, photographs, or other pictures from the date it was built. Compare them with what it looks like now, and then note any of the differences.

Evidence from the Building Itself

If the school is fairly old, there could be many clues about how differently students were treated in the past. For instance, some schools had separate entrances and playgrounds for girls and boys (you may still be able to spot the signs for "Girls" and "Boys" found above some doorways).

Find out what materials were used to build the school. Have they needed repairing or replacing? Make a list of features that have been altered. For instance, how was the school originally heated or lit, and what methods are used today?

Schools In the Air   *i*

A virtual school has no buildings at all! In remote areas of the United States, Canada, Australia, or southern Africa, students may learn at virtual schools. They work at home and communicate with teachers online or by phone.

Many old school buildings are still used today, like the building here (left), built in the late 19th century. Others (right) are brand new, using materials that are either new or more widely available in modern times, such as concrete or metal.

The Five Ws

Here is a graphic organizer to give you a broad picture of the areas you want to explore. Ask five simple questions: the five Ws:

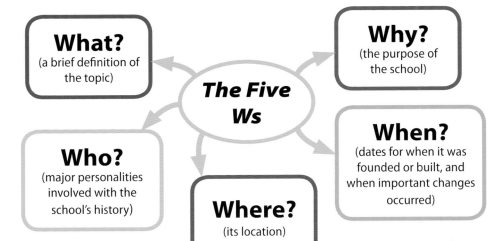

What?
(a brief definition of the topic)

Why?
(the purpose of the school)

The Five Ws

Who?
(major personalities involved with the school's history)

Where?
(its location)

When?
(dates for when it was founded or built, and when important changes occurred)

Written Evidence

When you begin research into your school, you should have a list of basic questions to give you a framework. How old are the main buildings? Have they been here since it was founded? What was on the site before? How have the buildings changed over the years? Many of the answers will be found in documents, held in the school itself or in libraries, museums, and local archives (for a more detailed list, see page 15). As usual, there are two kinds of documentary sources—primary sources and secondary sources:

- Primary sources: In the late 19th century, principals sometimes kept logbooks in which they recorded daily events and activities. Some also wrote daily diaries. Other records include punishment books (for noting punishments given to students, such as detention) and registers giving names of students who went to the school. Also, you can research some recent ex-students.

  Primary sources also include images. Your school may have many photographs—of classes or homerooms, of teachers, or of big events such as football games or school plays. Old maps show you how the area around the school has changed.

- Secondary sources: There may be references to your school in books, especially studies of the local area or of histories of education. Search in the online catalog of your local library. Stories involving your school will also have been published in the local newspaper. To find them, contact the newspaper itself or the library.

Eyewitness: Students Remember

If you have elderly relatives or family friends, ask them what school was like when they were young. They might remember having to use outhouses for bathrooms. They might also remember walking long distances to and from school each day—before kids could rely on buses or cars. You could learn a lot from these conversations.

1904.

Date	Name of pupil	Cause of Punishment	Nature of Punishment
Sept 27.	James Caine	Disobedience	3 stripes
"	James Young	do.	do.
"	Richd Johnstone	do.	do.
Nov. 9.	Harry S. Temple	Interfering with ball & caps	3 stripes -
Nov 28.	Robt Thos. Chapman	Fighting.	2 stripes sent to bed
"	William Reed	Quarrelling & tormenting other boys. Most insolent & defiant	Refused punishment. Very violent temper & Was suspended.

This is a page from a teacher's punishment book from the early 20th century. The headings to the table read (left to right): "Date," "Name of pupil [student]," "Cause of punishment," with the final column describing the actual punishment. "Stripes" means being hit by a rod or cane.

A Concept Web

A concept web is a type of graphic organizer. It is a neat way to set out your main areas for research on a single page. At the center of the web (like a spider web) is a bubble containing the main question you are trying to answer. Lines come out from it, each with a box containing a different source of information to use. And more lines branch out from these, with more detailed facts or suggestions. Here's how your concept web might look:

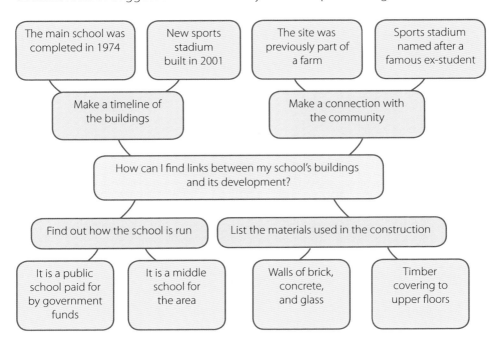

Living History

The story of your school can be found in people, too. Teachers past and present, as well as principals, parents, and students, will all have a lot to say about their time at the school. What were classes like? Did they have a particularly inspiring teacher? How did the buildings look? How much time was taken up with sports activities? What kind of punishments were there?

Such eyewitness accounts are another kind of primary source. But most of the material only exists in their memories, because it has never been written down. An important part of your research might be interviewing these people. Record what they say on tape or video, then transcribe (write down) the words to paper or a computer file. You will be creating a precious memory bank for the students who come after you.

Be Prepared

Make sure you are well prepared before you do the interviews. Have a list of questions already written down. Here are examples of what you could ask:

- What were school meals like?
- What were your sports colors?
- How strict were the teachers?
- What languages did you learn?
- What things did you do at recess?
- Where did many graduates go to college?

Making a Connection: Research and the Development of Education

You will learn a lot about your own school's past from this project. But it will also give you a much wider picture of how schools in general were run in years past. Try to connect the evidence you build up in your research to this wider picture. Many of the events (such as the introduction of new kinds of tests or the banning of physical punishment) may reflect changing attitudes. They will show how the education system—and society itself—has developed through time.

Teachers in 19th-century schools kept their students strictly in order. Any disobedient students might be punished with a beating.

Where Should I Look?:
Looking for Information Online

Everyone knows how quickly time flies when you are online. Here are some guidelines to help you find the material you want more efficiently:

- Be precise with your search. The more specific your search terms, the quicker you will reach a suitable web site.

- Check the date of the web site. A lot of information can become out of date quickly, as fresh research and evidence come to light. Use sites that have been recently updated.

- Check the source of the material. Anybody can build a web site and fill it with his or her own views. Look to see who produces the site and the person's motives for creating it. Ask yourself what kind of authority the writer has.

- Keep your concentration. It is very easy to be distracted by the glitter of online attractions. Stay focused on your topic and the original object of your research.

WHAT IS IT FOR?

In 1935, the U.S. government bought a run-down ironworks in the quiet countryside of Pennsylvania. It was called Hopewell, but the industrial buildings had been closed for over half a century and were mostly in ruins. A National Park Service historian, Roy Appleman, began the first detailed study of the place. At first, he found no one who knew much about its past.

Remembering the Past

Then, to Roy Appleman's astonishment, he got talking to 85-year-old Harker Long, who had lived in Hopewell many years before. Long had vivid memories of the place in its working days. In fact, as Appleman said later, "It is from Mr. Long that we have obtained practically all the information portraying Hopewell of an earlier day." So the first ideas for the restoration of the site were based largely on one man's recollections.

Today, at the central structure in Hopewell, there is a large white building in a well-kept grassy field. It has two long sloping roofs, and out of the middle sticks a big square chimney made of stone. Nearby are other stone and timber structures—sheds, barns, and houses. It is clearly an industrial site. But what is its purpose?

Take a Closer Look

Study the photograph. The wide stone building you can see does not look modern, even though it has been restored and cleaned up. It is probably at least 100 years old, and maybe much older. There are no workers to be seen, no smoke, and no vehicles, so it is obviously not in operation any longer. But what sort of industrial activity once went on inside it?

The big brick chimney gives us a clue. It suggests a powerful fire used to burn inside the building, and its smoke and fumes escaped through the chimney. You cannot see it, but inside the building is a tall stone structure connected to the bottom end of the chimney. It is shaped like a pyramid with a flattened top. What do you think this giant oven might have been used for?

brick chimney

Here, at the restored furnace house in Hopewell, you can
see a brick chimney to the left of the spire.

Where Should I Look?: Hopewell

If you visit Berks County, Pennsylvania, you can see Hopewell and
see the **furnace** for yourself. The grounds are open all year round.
The buildings are open throughout the summer, with more limited
access in winter. Otherwise, you can visit the official web site at
www.nps.gov/hofu/index.htm. Look in your local or school
library for books on the early Industrial Revolution. See page 38 for a
good starting point.

An Early Industrial Center

The oven was used for iron making. In Hopewell, this was called the Hopewell Furnace, which was in operation from 1771 to 1883. The fire heated iron **ore** (a mixture of iron with other minerals and impurities) to a very high temperature and turned it into cast iron. The iron was made into many products, including pots, tools, and stoves.

There were many other buildings, including a hearth for turning wood into **charcoal** (the furnace's main fuel), a **blacksmith**'s shop, and a waterwheel to drive the machinery. There were also houses, from the grand mansion where the ironmaster (boss) lived to boarding houses for the workers. Much of it has been restored and is now run by the National Parks Service.

Why Was It Built Here?

Early settlers in colonial North America urgently needed iron goods, such as tools, pots and pans, and many other items. It was very expensive to import these from Europe, so the settlers began building their own small ironworks. But these could only operate if the right natural resources were available. Iron-makers needed good local supplies of iron ore, **limestone**, and timber, as well as running water for mills.

Southeastern Pennsylvania had plenty of all these raw materials, and it soon became an important iron-producing region. By the time the Revolutionary War began in 1775, there were around 65 ironworks in the area. The Hopewell Furnace manufactured cannons and shot for the Continental (American) Army during the conflict.

The People of Hopewell

The population of Hopewell in the early 1800s was about 300. All of these people depended on the ironworks for their living. There were many jobs for the laborers, who usually worked 12-hour shifts. These are some of them:

- Woodcutters cut down trees for making charcoal.

- **Colliers** baked the timber in closed pits so it blackened and turned to charcoal.

- Miners dug the iron ore out of a nearby open pit and took limestone from quarries.

- **Teamsters** hauled the wood, ore, and limestone to the ironworks.

- Fillers loaded the furnace with the raw materials.

- Molders made the molds for the casts and filled them with molten metal.

A 19th-century blast furnace had to be regularly charged with fuel to keep it as hot as possible.

Zoom In: How the Blast Furnace Worked

The furnace burned day and night throughout most of the year. Workers raked away the ash and fed the fire with charcoal. The furnace was kept at a high heat by the blast of air from two pumps, driven by a wheel that was powered by running water. Twice an hour, fillers loaded the furnace from the top with iron ore and limestone. At a temperature of about 2,700 degrees Fahrenheit (1,500 degrees Celsius), the mixture melted. The limestone and the **oxygen** in the blasted air helped separate the pure iron metal from the impurities, which floated to the top and were skimmed off. Then the molten iron was ladled out into sand molds and left to cool.

Iron Changes the World

The development in iron making was one of the key factors in the Industrial Revolution. For thousands of years, wood and then charcoal were the main fuels used in smelting (purifying) iron ore. Then, in 1709, Englishman Abraham Darby began using **coke** instead. Coke is made from coal, by heating it in an oven. It was cheaper than charcoal and gave out more heat. The use of coke for smelting, along with other improvements such as the blast furnace (like the one at Hopewell), allowed high-quality iron to be produced more efficiently and cheaply.

The industry expanded rapidly, and the production of iron shot up. Iron was being used to make a huge variety of objects, from pipes and railroad tracks to bridges and steam engines. The new techniques spread to the United States and other parts of Europe.

Why Did Hopewell Furnace Close Down?

When coke took over from charcoal for smelting iron ore, Hopewell Furnace faced a crisis. Obviously, the company had to keep up with its rivals and change to the new fuel. But where would they get it? All the big new ironworks were being built in coal mining areas, but Hopewell was surrounded by woodland. The nearest mines were in northern Pennsylvania, which produced a type of coal called **anthracite**. In 1853, the owners of Hopewell built a second furnace to burn this new fuel. But they had left it too late, and the business never recovered, closing in 1883. The remains of the anthracite furnace can still be seen.

Making a Connection: The Industrial Revolution

The development of the Hopewell ironworks was just a small part of the gigantic leap forward in technology during the 1700s and 1800s, which we now call the Industrial Revolution. It began in Great Britain and spread to North America and parts of Europe. Industrialization created a huge increase in the production of goods, as new kinds of machines and processes were developed. It was also a social revolution, with huge numbers of people moving from the countryside to towns to work in factories, and the growth of railroads and other transportation systems.

The cheaper and more plentiful supply of iron made it possible to build many huge new structures. Here, it was used in the construction of a bridge in 1883.

Where Should I Look?: Looking at the Landscape

The landscape is full of the signs of old industrial activity. How do you go about finding these traces and identifying them? Archaeologists deal with the remains of ancient civilizations. Those who study old ironworks, mines, canals, factories, and similar places are called industrial archaeologists. They research the industries of the past, from the ancient world through the revolution of the 18th and 19th centuries right up to recent developments. Archaeological evidence includes buildings, machinery, transportation systems, and documents.

LIVED IN FOR A THOUSAND YEARS

In 1997, Saltford Manor House near Bath, England, was a wreck. Floors and ceilings had fallen in, and there were holes in the roof. Drains, water supply, and electricity were all in need of repair. The garden was a jungle. Many house hunters looked at it, but no one wanted to buy it.

Window on the Past

Then James Wynn and his family arrived. All they knew was that the house dated back to the 12th century and was in need of major restoration. Wynn was thrilled by what he saw. The walls were almost 4 feet (1.2 meters) thick, there were beautiful oak panels, carved oak beams, and a huge stone fireplace.

Most amazing of all was an ancient double window in one of the bedrooms, with fine columns and an arch with intricate zigzag carving. "I had never seen a window like this in any house," Wynn wrote later. The Wynn family bought the house and started the long and expensive process of restoring it and turning it into a home.

Making a Connection: The Normans in Britain

Duke William of Normandy (in present-day France) had conquered England after his famous victory at Hastings in 1066. This caused a major upheaval in English life. The duke became King William I and kept control over the country by imposing a new ruling class. He confiscated land from English nobles and gave it to his own French followers. The conquerors built a network of castles throughout England as military strongpoints. The legacy of the Norman invasion can still be widely seen in British life. There are many fine Norman buildings, including churches, towers, and castles. The English language contains many words derived from the French, and the Normans also altered the legal and social systems.

James Wynn transformed the ancient manor at Saltford
from a ruin into a beautiful home.

Searching For Clues

Wynn visited the library to discover more about Saltford Manor and its history.
He found the earliest mention of the manor, then just a wooden hall, before
the present house had been built. This came in the Domesday Book, a
survey of land and property in England made in 1086. The survey had been
ordered by King William I, the Norman ruler who had conquered the country
20 years earlier.

Wynn also used local records to learn the age of the beautiful bedroom
window. Architectural experts had recognized that it was almost identical to
arched windows in nearby Hereford Cathedral, which was completed in 1148.
Probably the same man had made both sets of windows. This dated at least
part of the present Saltford Manor to around 1148.

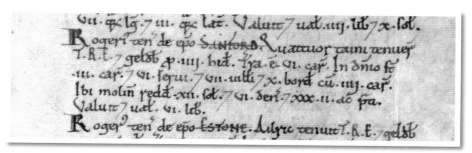

The original passage in the Domesday Book stated that there
was a timber manor house on the site in 1086.

Journey Through the Centuries

James Wynn's research took him from Norman times through most of English history. He found that Saltford Manor had connections with many great events, including:

1348 The deadly **plague** known as the Black Death swept across Britain. Many years later, a mass grave of plague victims was found near the manor.

1539 King Henry VIII ordered the closing of England's monasteries. Among them was Keynsham Abbey, the owner of the manor house. The abbey was stripped and destroyed.

1585 England was now a **Protestant** country, and all **Catholic** activity was banned. But in some places, priests still held Catholic services in secret. Saltford Manor was one of these, and it had Catholic owners. We know this because they built a hiding place next to the fireplace, where the priest could take refuge if danger threatened.

1642 The English Civil War broke out between the supporters of the king at the time, Charles I, and supporters of Parliament. The owner of Saltford Manor was then Lamorock Flower, who clearly opposed the king. Records show he donated one horse and its equipment to the Parliamentary army.

Research Road Show: Oldest in Europe?
Europe contains some of the most ancient buildings in the world:

- The Oldest Wooden House: Stone lasts much longer than timber, which can be rotted by damp or mold or eaten by insects. Yet the House of Bethlehem in Schwyz, Switzerland, was built entirely of wood, held together with wooden nails, back in 1287. It still stands today, although it is now a museum.

- The Oldest Town: In 2012, archaeologists began excavating a site at Provadia in Bulgaria. They found remains of houses, a burial ground, and city walls, which showed it was the oldest town in Europe— at least 6,000 years old.

- The Oldest Building: Discovered in 1840, the Tumulus of Bougon in western France contains a group of tombs that date back to about 4800 BCE. This makes them probably among the most ancient structures in the world.

The Norman window at Saltford Manor was ornately carved with zigzag patterns on the arch.

Who Lived Here Before?

Wynn did not just research the fabric of the house; he also uncovered the lives of previous owners. Over the centuries, many different families had lived in Saltford Manor. Among the first was Robert Fitzroy, an illegitimate son of England's King Henry I. When Robert died in 1147, his son William commissioned the double window as a **memorial**.

Next came the Rodneys, who were also in the service of the monarch, and who owned the manor for over 300 years. After them, the Flower family worked hard over the next 300 years, extending and modernizing the building and developing the farmland. But by the 1920s, agriculture was in decline and the Flower family left Saltford altogether. The manor was then rented to a local farmer.

War and Decay

The story of Saltford Manor had now reached World War II. From talking to local people and reading newspaper articles, James Wynn learned that about 100 children arrived in the village as **evacuees** in 1939. They had been sent from London to keep them safe from German bombing raids. Several came to live at the manor.

After the war, the Flower family decided they would sell the manor, which was now run-down and shabby. Wynn found the real estate agent's advertisement for the sale in 1946. The property was described as "Saltford Manor Farm, comprising the interesting and reputed 16th century Manor House (at present in disrepair)."

Zoom In:
Looking at Different Types of Maps

Different maps of the same area through history can show you important details of how it has changed. This is especially important when researching the development of one particular house. The maps will show how boundary lines, paths, roads, and waterways have gradually altered, and when new buildings were added. There are many kinds of maps to be found in libraries and records offices:

- Old maps: Before about 1750, maps were not very accurately drawn. However, many showed buildings in elevation (as seen from the ground), which can make it easier to identify them and know what they look like.

- U.S. Geological Survey: The USGS was set up in 1879 to map and record the vast area of the United States. It produces many series of historic maps, dating from the late 19th century, many available online at **nationalmap.gov/historical/**

- Fire insurance maps: From the late 18th century, insurance companies mapped urban areas, giving large-scale details of buildings (mainly industrial or retail). You can find these in your local library. The best-known of these are the Sanborn Maps, which you can look at here: **www.sanborn.com**

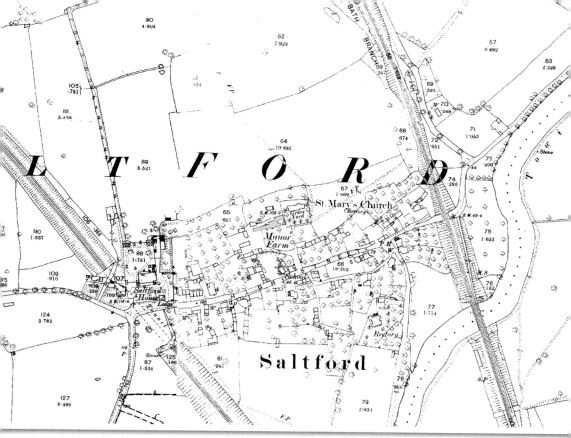

This is an old map of Saltford, England. What can you tell about the surrounding area when you look at a map like this?

Fame Comes to Saltford

Meanwhile, other people were interested in the history of the manor house. In 2003, the magazine *Country Life* organized a competition to find the oldest continuously inhabited house in Great Britain. The judge was architectural historian John Goodall, who researched all the houses submitted.

Goodall decided that Saltford, with its Norman window dating from about 1148, was the winner. It was officially the longest lived-in building in the country. Suddenly, the ancient home was famous. Newspaper reporters and TV news crews flocked to interview the Wynns and photograph the manor. James Wynn told them, "You get a wonderful sense of history. I can look at [centuries of] architecture before I brush my teeth."

THE STATUE OF LIBERTY

On an island at the entrance to New York Harbor stands a giant copper statue. It is the figure of a robed woman holding a torch high above her head. The statue towers on top of a massive granite pedestal, and is over 300 feet (nearly 93 meters) high overall. It is the Statue of Liberty, and it is one of the most famous landmarks in the world.

The Statue of Liberty stands on Liberty Island at the entrance to New York Harbor. It faces out to sea to greet incoming ships. In the background of this photograph, behind the statue, you can see Ellis Island, where **immigrants** from the ships came to register with officials.

Is There Anything New to Learn?

Some buildings have very obvious links to history, requiring only a small amount of detective work to find out about their past. The Statue of Liberty is one well-known example. It was built for a very clear purpose, its story is well documented, and it is easy to find out about.

Yet new discoveries have still been made. One of the most important was in 1985, nearly 100 years after the statue was first erected. The source of the copper sheets that covered the statue had always been a mystery. Then scientists from Bell Laboratories analyzed two copper fragments—one from the statue, and one from Visnes mine in Norway. They matched, and the old mystery was solved.

A Celebration of Liberty

The idea for the statue came from a French politician and writer named Edouard de Laboulaye. He admired the United States, and especially the U.S. **Constitution**, which promoted the ideal of liberty for all its citizens. He had been a big supporter of President Abraham Lincoln in the struggle to abolish slavery, which finally succeeded in 1865.

That same year, de Laboulaye proposed that the people of France and the United States should erect a joint monument to honor the American achievement. It would celebrate the ideals of justice, freedom, and democracy for all. Inspired by de Laboulaye, French sculptor Auguste Bartholdi proposed this monument should be a massive statue to be called "Liberty Enlightening the World."

Making a Connection: France and the United States

This was a turbulent period for both the United States and France. The long and bloody Civil War in the United States ended in 1865, and then President Lincoln was assassinated. Despite this tragedy, the United States was still a democratic country, and slavery had ended. France, on the other hand, was ruled by an emperor, Napoleon III, who controlled much of the government. In 1870, France suffered a disastrous defeat in the war against Prussia, and there was a popular uprising against Napoleon III. De Laboulaye saw the United States as a beacon of liberty—in contrast to his own country at the time.

Making the Statue

Bartholdi set to work on the sculpture in 1875. It was made in 300 separate pieces. Each piece was produced in four stages:

1. A strong wooden frame was built.
2. Plaster was applied to the frame, making a full-scale model.
3. Workers made a wooden form that followed exactly the shape of the plaster model.
4. Sheets of copper were bent and hammered over the form.

The statue was so huge that it needed a special framework inside for support. This was designed by Gustave Eiffel (builder of the Eiffel Tower in Paris). He erected an iron tower at the center of the sculpture, which was connected to the copper covering with a system of iron bars. It was very strong, but also flexible enough to allow the whole structure to move slightly. This meant it could react to changes in wind or temperature without being damaged.

Crossing the Atlantic—In Pieces

A year later, the first section of the sculpture (the arm holding the torch) was ready. It was sent to an exhibition in Philadelphia to help raise funds, before being returned to France. Bit by bit, the finished parts were collected in Paris and assembled. The complete statue was officially presented to the American people on July 4, 1884.

But first, it had to be transported across the Atlantic Ocean to its new home. So the statue was dismantled again, and the pieces were packed in crates aboard a ship. The vessel arrived at New York on June 17, 1885. On October 28, 1886, the sculpture was unveiled. There were parades on land and sea, and over one million New Yorkers watched the ceremony.

Research Road Show: A Colossal Statue

The word "colossal" comes from the Latin word *colossus*, which means an enormous statue or monument. The most famous Colossus spanned the entrance to the harbor of Rhodes, Greece. Built in about 290 BCE, it was 105 feet (32 meters) high and one of the Seven Wonders of the World. It was destroyed in an earthquake in 226 BCE, but the ruins have never been found.

The Statue of Liberty was put together using scaffolding. This happened in Paris before it was finally shipped to where it now stands in New York City.

Zoom In: What Do the Various Details Mean?

The statue represents Libertas, the Roman goddess of Freedom. But she is more than just a giant figure. The sculpture includes several symbols that represent ideas and events in history:

- A broken **shackle** and chain lie by the figure's feet. These signify the end of slavery in the United States after it was abolished in 1865.

- Liberty holds a stone tablet in her left hand. It is inscribed with the date July 4, 1776, when the United States declared independence from Great Britain.

- The torch in her right hand represents enlightenment (the light of understanding and freedom).

- Her crown has seven spikes. These are rays of light and probably symbols of the seven continents of the world.

A Welcome Sight

As soon as it was completed, the Statue of Liberty became a very special landmark. Between 1886 and 1924, nearly 14 million immigrants passed the statue when their ships entered New York Harbor. Many more arrived after World War II. They had come from Europe and other parts of the world to settle in the United States and find a new life. The giant figure was a symbol of welcome.

Its importance to immigrants was recognized in 1903, when a new plaque was added to the pedestal of the statue. It was inscribed with a poem by Emma Lazarus called *The New Colossus*, which celebrated the comforting image of the statue. The poem's most famous lines read:

> *"...give me your tired, your poor,*
> *Your huddled masses yearning to breathe free,*
> *The wretched refuse of your teeming shore.*
> *Send these, the homeless, tempest-tost to me,*
> *I lift my lamp beside the golden door!"*

Looking After a Landmark

In 1933, the National Park Service (NPS) took over the running of the statue and its island. By now, it was looking shabby and overgrown. The NPS cleared away old military buildings, planted new trees, and laid paved walkways. When this program was completed in 1956, Bedloe's Island was renamed Liberty Island. Today, a boat links Liberty Island with the nearby Ellis Island, which houses a museum dedicated to the immigration experience into New York City.

Making a Connection: Landing on Ellis Island

Once past Liberty Island, the immigrant ships came to Ellis Island. Between 1892 and 1924, this was the first stop for more than 12 million immigrants to the United States. They were examined and registered, a process that took from three to seven hours. Those accepted were taken onto the mainland. Anyone refused entry (such as a convicted criminal) was sent back to the country he or she came from. Ellis Island became part of the Statue of Liberty National Monument in 1965.

By 1982, the statue needed major restoration. Scaffolding was put up around the structure and work began. A new torch, glittering with gold leaf, was made to replace the old one. The copper skin was cleaned and repaired. The iron bars in the framework were replaced with stainless steel. A new elevator was fitted inside to carry passengers up to the viewing platform in the crown. The project was completed in time to celebrate the statue's centenary (100th anniversary) in 1986.

Eyewitness: An Immigrant Sees the Statue

"I was 16 when I passed the Statue of Liberty. It was an early morning sunrise when I first saw her. Everyone standing on the boat was very excited. She gave me a comforting feeling, that I was here, I made it, I had arrived. She seemed so personal to me."

Carla Montague, who came to New York from East Germany in 1956

The first sight of the Statue of Liberty was a moment of celebration for most immigrants arriving into the United States.

THE GLORY OF ST. PANCRAS

In 1998, a major project was underway to restore St. Pancras railroad station in London, England, to its original glory. As part of its conservation, expert Helen Hughes was asked to find out what color the vast iron roof **trusses** had been painted when the station was built in the 1860s. Her tests showed the trusses had first been colored brown so that they would not show dirt from the steam trains, but later they had been repainted blue. Hughes re-created that blue paint, and today the soaring trusses are the same color as the sky.

A 19th-Century Station

Millions of people pass through railroad stations every year. But few notice the station buildings or wonder how, when, and why they were constructed. St. Pancras station is worth a closer look. It is not only a complex and magnificent building, but also one that contains an extraordinary history.

The station was built in the second half of the 19th century, when the United Kingdoms's railroads were run by private companies. One of these, the Midland Railway, began laying a new line between Bedford and London, in England, in 1864. The line would end in the area known as St. Pancras, where the company planned a grand new **terminus** station. First, a space had to be cleared to build it in. This meant evicting 10,000 people and demolishing seven streets of houses. A church had to be moved, as well as 10,000 coffins from its graveyard.

The Great Train Shed

St. Pancras is the grandest station ever built in Great Britain. The central part is the platform complex, with a huge single-span roof (without central supports). This amazing "train shed" was designed by William Barlow, as the covered area where long passenger trains pulled in. It is 689 feet (210 meters) long, 243 feet (75 meters) wide, and 100 feet (30 meters) high. Barlow's roof, built of iron and glass, was the largest single-span structure in the world at that time.

In 1873, a second great piece of architecture was added. This was the Midland Grand Hotel, a huge four-story building designed by leading architect George Gilbert Scott. It was built in the "Neo-Gothic" (New Gothic) style, which was popular at the time. This was a revival of the Gothic architecture of the Middle Ages, which had produced many great churches and other buildings in Western Europe. The hotel's many spires, the turreted clock tower, and ornate windows and chimneys all give it a medieval look.

The sweeping front of St. Pancras station and hotel was decorated with stone columns, patterns in the brickwork, and small spires on top. This part of the building is built in a "Neo-Gothic" style, which was popular at the time.

The Rise of Railroads

In the mid-19th century, railroads were booming in Great Britain. By the 1860s and 1870s, this was also true in the United States. In 1862, Congress passed the Pacific Railway Act, which led to a "transcontinental railroad." This linked the eastern and western parts of the country in ways never possible before. Find out more about the rise of railroads on web sites such as **www.loc.gov/ teachers/classroommaterials/presentationsandactivities/ presentations/timeline/riseind/railroad** or look in the transportation history section of your library.

In October 1940, a German bomb fell through the roof of the train shed, wrecking locomotives, train carriages, and some track.

Bombs on St. Pancras

World War I (1914–1918) was mostly fought outside of Great Britain. But war struck Britain on the moonless night of February 17, 1918, when a lone German aircraft dropped a bomb directly onto St. Pancras station. Many civilians and railroad workers were taking shelter beneath the entrance arch (as was the typical practice during air raids in London), and 20 of them were killed. Another raid damaged the train shed itself.

In World War II (1939–1945), German bombers also targeted St. Pancras station during the "Blitz" period of September 1940 to May 1941. Five bombs hit the station, causing massive damage to several platforms. One bomb smashed through the floor and down into the subway tunnel beneath. It exploded there and completely blocked the line. It took a week to clear away the rubble—and another bomb that had failed to explode also had to be cleared away.

Soldiers and Evacuees

St. Pancras was a meeting point for soldiers, sailors, and airmen, including many troops from the United States and other **Allied** countries. They passed through the station on their way to and from training camps in Britain, or to the coast to board ships headed for the fighting. Numbers of servicemen on the move increased in the buildup to the invasion of France in June 1944.

Many children came to St. Pancras in the weeks just before and after the outbreak of war in September 1939. Crowds of boys and girls, often upset about leaving home, were herded onto the platforms and sent by train away from London. These children were called evacuees. Their parents believed they would be safer from bombs in the country than in the capital.

Saved!

By the 1960s, St. Pancras was looking shabby. Its great glass roof was patched and filthy and let in little sunlight. Many trains now went to nearby stations instead. The Midland Grand Hotel had closed down and was being used as offices for railroad workers. Plans were made to demolish the hotel altogether and build a modern office building.

However, in 1962, the English poet John Betjeman started a campaign to save the building. He glorified the station as "that cluster of towers and **pinnacles**...and the great arc of Barlow's engine shed gaping to devour incoming engines." Joined by many others, Betjeman succeeded in having St. Pancras classed as a Grade 1 listed building in 1967. This meant it could not be destroyed.

A New Life

During the 1990s, a program began to return St. Pancras to its former glory. First, the exterior of the hotel building was repaired and restored. Then, in 2004, the interior was completely redeveloped, and it reopened as a hotel and apartments in 2011.

Meanwhile, the station itself had an even grander future. It was selected to be the terminus for the new Eurostar rail line linking Britain with the European mainland through the Channel Tunnel. Costing well over $1.2 billion and given a new name (St. Pancras International), the station was officially reopened in 2007. Among the new features was a statue of John Betjeman.

Making a Connection: It's Greener By Rail

Trains are one of the most efficient forms of transportation ever invented. A railroad locomotive can haul enormous weights and save fuel. One train can carry as much cargo as 300 trucks. This is because train wheels run on smooth metal rails, which create less friction (drag) than roads. Electric trains are also much cleaner; they produce 10 times less carbon dioxide (or CO_2—carbon dioxide is the gas that is a major cause of global warming) than an aircraft making the same journey.

A statue of the poet John Betjeman stands on a platform of the recently renovated St. Pancras train shed. Betjeman was part of the effort in the 1960s to save the building.

Where Should I Look?

Railroad buildings such as St. Pancras station are a rich source of history. Learn about the development of mass transportation and how it has changed society, as well as the scientific story of railroads, from the steam locomotive to the modern bullet train.

- Most libraries have a good section on railroads and transportation history.

- Look online. For a wide-ranging history, go to **memory.loc.gov/ammem/gmdhtml/rrhtml/rrintro.html**

- Go to your local station. Are the buildings old or new? When was the line built?

- Many railroad lines and stations have closed in the last 50 years. Why has this happened? Perhaps you can investigate. Also, look on maps and explore your neighborhood.

TIMELINE

This timeline sets out some of the world's most famous and exciting structures in chronological order. There are brief descriptions of those you may not be familiar with. Buildings heavily featured in the main text are marked in **bold**.

BCE

c. 4800	Tumulus of Bougon, France
c. 2750	Stonehenge, United Kingdom
c. 2600	Great Pyramid of Khufu, Egypt
c. 1700	Palace at Knossos, Crete (the center of the Minoan civilization)
447	**Parthenon, Athens, Greece**
214	Great Wall of China
19	Herod's Temple, Palestine (the second great Jewish temple in Jerusalem)

CE

70	Colosseum, Rome, Italy (huge arena used for games and gladiator fights)
532	Church of Hagia Sofia, Istanbul, Turkey (the greatest Byzantine church, now a museum)
c. 1065	Westminster Abbey, London, United Kingdom
1132	**Rievaulx Abbey, United Kingdom**
1140	Temples at Angkor Wat, Cambodia (the largest Hindu temple complex in the world)
c. 1145	Chartres Cathedral, France (Christian church thought to be an outstanding example of Gothic architecture)
c. 1150	**Saltford Manor, United Kingdom**
1338	Alhambra Palace, Spain (the palace and fortress in the city of Granada, built for the Moorish sultan)
c. 1500	Machu Picchu, Peru (Inca city built high on a mountain ridge)
1599	Globe Theatre, London, United Kingdom (theater where William Shakespeare wrote and acted)
1630	Taj Mahal, India
c. 1675	St. Paul's Cathedral, London, United Kingdom
1771	**Hopewell Furnace, Pennsylvania, United States**
1782	Monticello, Charlottesville, Virginia, United States (the home of President Thomas Jefferson, who designed the home himself)
1793	Capitol, Washington, D.C., United States
1800	White House, Washington, D.C., United States
1866	**St. Pancras station, London, United Kingdom**

1869	Brooklyn Bridge, New York City, United States
1886	**Statue of Liberty, New York City, United States**
1887	Eiffel Tower, Paris, France
1894	Reichstag, Berlin, Germany (the German parliament building, restored after reunification in 1990)
1910	Pennsylvania Station, New York City, United States
1928	Chrysler Building, New York City, United States (Art Deco skyscraper)
1955	Hiroshima Peace Center, Japan (community center and museum in memory of those killed by the first nuclear bomb)
1966	World Trade Center, New York City, United States (building destroyed in the attacks of September 11, 2001)
1973	Sydney Opera House, Australia
1989	Louvre Pyramid, Paris, France (the opening of a glass pyramid at the entrance to this famous art museum. The museum was opened before this date.)
1997	Guggenheim Museum, Bilbao, Spain (art museum with innovative curved walls)
2004	Millau Viaduct, France (one of the highest bridges in the world, which spans the Tarn Valley)

Timeline: Education

These are some of the key dates in the history of schools and education in the United States.

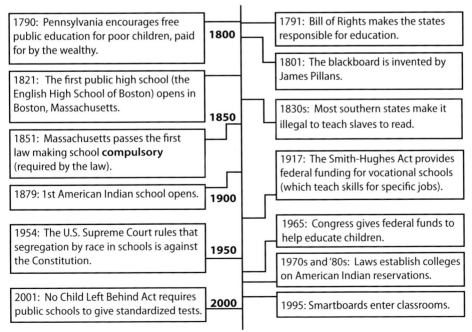

1790: Pennsylvania encourages free public education for poor children, paid for by the wealthy.

1800

1791: Bill of Rights makes the states responsible for education.

1801: The blackboard is invented by James Pillans.

1821: The first public high school (the English High School of Boston) opens in Boston, Massachusetts.

1850

1830s: Most southern states make it illegal to teach slaves to read.

1851: Massachusetts passes the first law making school **compulsory** (required by the law).

1917: The Smith-Hughes Act provides federal funding for vocational schools (which teach skills for specific jobs).

1879: 1st American Indian school opens.

1900

1954: The U.S. Supreme Court rules that segregation by race in schools is against the Constitution.

1950

1965: Congress gives federal funds to help educate children.

1970s and '80s: Laws establish colleges on American Indian reservations.

2001: No Child Left Behind Act requires public schools to give standardized tests.

2000

1995: Smartboards enter classrooms.

GLOSSARY

abolish put an end to something

allied describes members of a group, an alliance. This can be used to describe those fighting with the US in World War I and World War II.

anthracite hard type of coal that burns very cleanly

archaeology scientific study of the remains of past ages

archive place where documents or other materials of historical importance are kept safe

artifact tool, weapon, or other object produced by humans

blacksmith someone who heats and shapes iron with a hammer

bushel unit used to measure dry goods

Catholic belonging to the version of the Christian faith headed by the pope in Rome

census official counting of the population and collection of other statistics

charcoal black fuel made by heating wood to dry it and get rid of certain chemicals

clapboard wall covering of wooden boards or tiles

classical belonging to ancient Greek or Roman culture

coke fuel made by baking coal to get rid of chemicals that prevent it from burning cleanly

collier person who works to produce coal or charcoal

compulsory required or necessary

conservation act of protecting and repairing something

constitution laws and principles that make up a system of government

democracy system of government in which the people of a country freely elect their own rulers

evacuee person sent away from a dangerous or threatened area

evidence in history, anything that helps create an accurate picture of the past

furnace chamber in which fuel is burned to produce heat

immigrant someone who enters another country to settle permanently

interpretation explanation of the meaning of something

limestone type of rock, used in building as well as iron-making

memorial something designed as a way to remember the dead

minaret tall, thin tower on a mosque from which Muslims are called to prayer

missionary person who goes on a mission (usually to do religious work in a foreign country)

monastery place where monks live

monument building or other structure erected as a memorial to a person or event

ore mixture of minerals found naturally in the ground, from which one valuable mineral (such as iron) is extracted

oxygen colorless gas that makes up 21 percent of the atmosphere and that is necessary to life

pagan someone who does not follow any of the major religious faiths

patron goddess goddess who is believed to protect and support a city or country

pediment wide gable (triangular space) on the end of a Grecian building

pinnacle small, pointed spire on the roof of a building

plague highly infectious epidemic disease

primary source historical source that dates from the period itself

Protestant belonging to a version of the Christian faith that is separate from the Roman Catholic Church

replica exact copy of something

secondary source historical source produced somewhat after the event

shackle metal lock that fastens around an ankle or wrist, attached to a chain

symbol something that represents or stands for something else (usually a material object that stands for an idea)

teamster someone who drives a team of horses

terminus end of a railroad line

truss framework which helps keep a structure upright

FIND OUT MORE

Books

Many of the buildings in this book have other books written about them already. Some interesting reads about these buildings and other great architecture are:

Kerns, Ann. *Seven Wonders of Architecture* (Seven Wonders). Minneapolis: Twenty-First Century, 2010.

Nardo, Don. *Architecture* (Eye on Art). Detroit: Lucent, 2008.

Ricciuti, Edward R. *America's Top 100*. Woodbridge, Conn.: Blackbirch, 2000.

Roeder, Annette. *13 Buildings Children Should Know*. New York: Prestel, 2009.

Schmidt, Thomas, and Michael Lewis. *National Geographic's Guide to America's Historic Places*. Washington, D.C.: National Geographic Society, 1997.

Simon, Garfield. *On the Map: A Mind-Expanding Exploration of the Way the World Looks*. New York: Gotham, 2013.

Stevenson, Neil. *Architecture Explained*. New York: Dorling Kindersley, 2007.

Web Sites

In addition to those shown below, it is good to visit the web sites mentioned elsewhere in this book. Also use a search engine to find more information about similar or nearby buildings featured in this book.

www.archkidecture.org
Find imaginative ideas on how to engage with the buildings around you.

www.historicplaces.net
This web site offers a register of many historic places in the United States and Canada, listed by state and region or category.

www.nps.gov/stli/index.htm
Learn more about the Statue of Liberty at this site, which includes a virtual tour of the statue.

www.nypl.org/audiovideo/how-research-building
This video outlines how to research buildings in New York City using libraries and other resources.

www.pbs.org/opb/historydetectives/technique/building-background
Find tips on how to investigate the history of a building.

www.pbs.org/opb/timeteam/
This is the web site for a live TV archaeology program called *Time Team*.

Further Research

The history of buildings is a huge subject. There is much more to find out and lots of sources to look through. Try to find out more about one of these other topics:

- Houses in fiction: Many characters in stories live in real houses—or otherwise make-believe versions of them. There is the Little House on the Prairie in the Midwest (Laura Ingalls Wilder) or Nathaniel Hawthorne's House of Seven Gables in Salem, Massachusetts. Think of more, and find out where the buildings are located and what their real histories are.

- Explore great buildings: Somewhere near you will be an important government building, a beautiful religious building, or a historic house. Visit several of these places and compare them to see how grand architecture developed through different periods. Sometimes there might even be different styles of architecture in a place, where things have changed throughout the years. Perhaps further research at a local library or at a local museum will help inform your knowledge of the local architecture, too.

- What is the oldest building in your town or city? Use research methods (such as those mentioned above but also elsewhere in this book) to discover which local structure has the longest history. How has it changed over time?

INDEX